THE THIRD—AN
BEST—637 BEST T
EVER

"It has been my experience that folks who
have no vices have very few virtues."
Abraham Lincoln (1809–1865)

"The opposite of talking isn't listening.
The opposite of talking is waiting."
Fran Lebowitz

"Diplomacy is the art of saying 'Nice
doggie' until you can find a rock."
Will Rogers (1879–1935)

"As Miss America, my goal is to bring
peace to the entire world and then to get
my own apartment."
Jay Leno

THE THIRD
AND POSSIBLY THE BEST

637

BEST THINGS
ANYBODY EVER SAID

Illustrated by old line cuts, many of which
are quite amusing

Again chosen and arranged by
ROBERT BYRNE
Who bent over backwards

FAWCETT CREST • NEW YORK

For
Susan Richman
The best in the business

Thou shalt not steal.
Exodus 20:15
(ca. 700 B.C.)

CONTENTS

✎◉●◉✎

Introduction

PART ONE

Religion, Life Itself, Men and Women, Cats, Clothes, Love, Sex, Marriage, Self-Abuse, Parents, Kids, Work, Money, Crime, Old Age, Death, and one thing and another

PART TWO

Cynicism, Happiness, Morality, Bores, Food, Doctors, Parties, Alcohol, Music, Sports, Art, Law, Travel, Airplanes, Science, War, Movies, Politics, Presidents, Writers, and various odds and ends

PART THREE

Miscellaneous

Sources, References, and Notes

Index of Authors

Index of Subjects and Key Words

INTRODUCTION

The first volume in this series appeared in 1982 and was called *The 637 Best Things Anybody Ever Said*. The title, I hoped, would provoke bookstore browsers into sampling the contents, after which they would be compelled to read a few lines to the cashier while fishing for their wallets. The number 637 was not entirely arbitrary—that's how many good quotes were left after I boiled down my own notebooks and gutted other people's collections. The book presented what I thought were the tastiest morsels from the world's wags and wits. Although I asked to hear from readers on the off chance that I might have missed something, I gave little thought to a sequel. A second serving, I felt sure, would be bland by comparison.

Well, a year later I was one red-faced compiler! I had continued compulsively jotting down good lines—once the eyes and ears are awakened to the possibilities they can't be put back to sleep—and readers were stuffing my mailbox with bon mots I had overlooked, some of them their own. Asking for contributions from readers, like the Treaty of Versailles following World War I, had turned out to be a tragic mistake that made a sequel inevitable.

The Other 637 Best Things Anybody Ever Said was published in 1984 and is one of the few sequels since the New Testament that is as good as the original, perhaps better in that it contains fewer of my own lines. It sold twice as many copies as the prequel, resulting in twice as many suggestions from readers and teaching me that the path to success in the literary world may lie in producing the same book over and over. I don't know about you, but when I hear or read a good line I can hardly wait to tell it to somebody else, so here I am again. I never would have believed four years ago that a third volume was possible or that I would be more or less forced by a sense of duty and money to compile it.

The number 637 has turned out to be more a measure of the narrowness of my original vision than an index of the world's wit and insight. Still, it is a pretty good number for a quote book designed to be read from cover to cover; bigger and the reader's eyes would begin to glaze, smaller and it would be hard to get published in hardcover.

It's amazing how much funny stuff there is. Funny people are everywhere, and not all of them belong to the army of some three thousand standup comedians now terrorizing America; some, in fact, have been dead for hundreds of years. Then there are the ordinary people who are funny only now and then, a point not interesting enough to pursue. In any event, a river of rich comedic milk is flowing across the land, and as fast as I skim off the cream more cream appears. That's fine for you, but I may be doomed to wade around forever in other people's pith. Not that it's such a bad life. I can go to a comedy club and deduct it as a business expense.

I considered calling this collection *The Third and Possibly the Last 637 Best Things Anybody Ever Said*, but I didn't want to have to eat those words as I have so many others. Like H. L. Mencken (1880–1956) before me, what I really want to do is write a book that weighs at least five pounds. I'll work on it between trips to the mailbox.

A few announcements. Dates are given only for people who strike me as being dead; others can fend for themselves. In Parts One and Two, quotes are grouped in rough, untitled categories. Use the indexes of subjects and authors if you want to locate a half-remembered quote. To facilitate reading in the normal front-to-back manner, categories generally follow one another in logical rather than alphabetical order . . . for example, Marriage follows Sex and Self-Abuse follows Marriage. In most books of this kind, Sex is followed by such unrelated topics as Shakespeare, Sickness, and Socialism, and there is no category for Self-Abuse at all. I'm uneasy about crediting lines to certain celebrities, for I sense the touch of the gag-writer's hidden hand. It would contribute to accuracy and completeness if those ghosts would step forward and identify themselves even if it costs them their jobs. Unless you are familiar with all three volumes, don't write to point out anything. Finally, some quotes are not numbered because they appeared earlier in the series ("Plato was a bore"), and quotes used more than once in the following pages are numbered on first appearance only ("Hemingway was a jerk").

Have fun—I did.

Robert Byrne
% Fawcett Books
201 E. 50th Street
New York, New York 10022

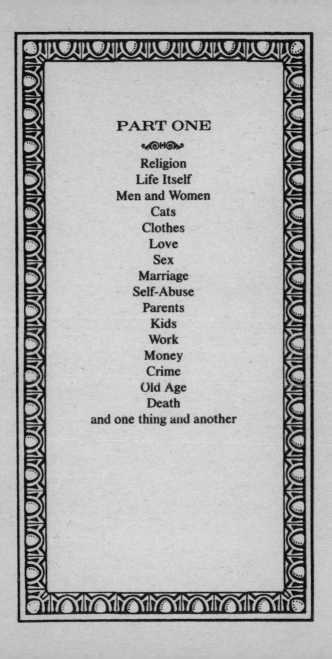

PART ONE

Religion
Life Itself
Men and Women
Cats
Clothes
Love
Sex
Marriage
Self-Abuse
Parents
Kids
Work
Money
Crime
Old Age
Death
and one thing and another

1

The only thing that stops God from sending another flood is that the first one was useless.

Nicholas Chamfort (1741–1794)

2

The world is proof that God is a committee.

Bob Stokes

3

God is dead, but fifty thousand social workers have risen to take his place.   *J.D. McCoughey*

4

Which is it, is man one of God's blunders or is God one of man's?   *Friedrich Nietzsche (1844–1900)*

5

Nietzsche was stupid and abnormal.

Leo Tolstoy (1828–1910)

6

Millions long for immortality who don't know what to do on a rainy Sunday afternoon. *Susan Ertz*

7

A pious man is one who would be an atheist if the king were. *Jean de La Bruyère (1645–1696)*

8

I detest converts almost as much as I do missionaries.

H.L. Mencken (1880–1956)

9

Most of my friends are not Christians, but I have some who are Anglicans or Roman Catholics.

Dame Rose Macaulay (1881–1958)

10

Promise me that if you become a Christian you'll become a Presbyterian. *Lord Beaverbrook (1879–1964) to Josef Stalin in 1941*

11

The history of saints is mainly the history of insane people.   *Benito Mussolini (1883–1945)*

12

In Burbank there's a drive-in church called Jack-in-the-Pew. You shout your sins into the face of a plastic priest.
Johnny Carson

13

When I was a kid in the ghetto, a gang started going around harassing people, so some of the toughest kids formed a gang called The Sharks to stop them. The other gang was called The Jehovah's Witnesses.
Charles Kosar

14

Jesus was a Jew, yes, but only on his mother's side.
Archie Bunker

15

Unless you hate your father and mother and wife and brothers and sisters and, yes, even your own life, you can't be my disciple.   *Jesus Christ (0?–32?), if St. Luke is to be believed. See Luke 14:26.*

Jesus was a crackpot.   *Bhagwan Shree Rajneesh*

Let Bhagwans be Bhagwans.   *Headline considered by the* Washington Post

Jesus died too soon. If he had lived to my age he would have repudiated his doctrine.
    Friedrich Nietzsche (1844–1900)

Nietzsche was stupid and abnormal.
    Leo Tolstoy (1828–1910)

I'm not going to climb into the ring with Tolstoy.
    Ernest Hemingway (1898–1961)

Hemingway was a jerk.   *Harold Robbins*

21

The purpose of life is a life of purpose.   *Robert Byrne*

22

I like life. It's something to do.   *Ronnie Shakes*

23

Life is divided into the horrible and the miserable.
Woody Allen

24

Life is just a bowl of pits.   *Rodney Dangerfield*

25

Life being what it is, one dreams of revenge.
Paul Gauguin (1848–1903)

26

If I had my life to live over, I'd live over a delicatessen.
Unknown

27

Man is more an ape than many of the apes.
Friedrich Nietzsche (1844–1900)

Neitzsche was stupid and abnormal.
Leo Tolstoy (1828–1910)

28

He who looketh upon a woman loseth a fender.
Sign in auto repair shop

Mahatma Gandhi was what wives wish their husbands were: thin, tan, and moral.   *Unknown*

The only time a woman really succeeds in changing a man is when he's a baby.   *Natalie Wood (1938–1981)*

I'm a disgrace to my sex. I should work in an Arabian palace as a eunuch.   *Woody Allen*

Girls are always running through my mind. They don't dare walk.   *Andy Gibb*

One good thing about being a man is that men don't have to talk to each other.   *Peter Cocotas*

Of all the wild beasts of land or sea, the wildest is woman.   *Menander (342?–291? B.C.)*

35

A woman is always buying something.

Ovid (43 B.C.–A.D. *18)*

36

Nothing is more intolerable than a wealthy woman.

Juvenal (60?–140?)

37

A woman talks to one man, looks at a second, and thinks of a third.   *Bhartrihari, ca. 625*

38

Woman was God's second mistake.

Friedrich Nietzsche (1844–1900)

Nietzsche was stupid and abnormal.

Leo Tolstoy (1828–1910)

39

Women speak two languages, one of which is verbal.

Steve Rubenstein

40

Women who seek to be equal with men lack ambition.
Timothy Leary

41

Women are like elephants to me. I like to look at them but I wouldn't want to own one.
W.C. Fields (1880–1946)

42

Phyllis Schlafly speaks for all American women who oppose equal rights for themselves.   *Andy Rooney*

43

Housework can kill you if done right.

Erma Bombeck

44

What do women want? Shoes.   *Mimi Pond*

45

Shopping tip: You can get shoes for 85 cents at bowling alleys.   *Al Clethen*

46

Can you imagine a world without men? No crime and lots of happy fat women.   *Sylvia (Nicole Hollander)*

47

Veni, vidi, Visa. *(We came, we saw, we went shopping.)*
Jan Barrett

48

Any girl can be glamorous; all you have to do is stand still and look stupid.   *Hedy Lamarr*

49

If they could put one man on the moon, why can't they put them all?   *Unknown*

50

Good breeding consists of concealing how much we think of ourselves and how little we think of the other person. *Mark Twain (1835–1910)*

51

Charm is a way of getting the answer yes without asking a clear question. *Albert Camus (1913–1960)*

52

Good taste is the worst vice ever invented.
Dame Edith Sitwell (1887–1964)

53

We are all born charming, fresh, and spontaneous and must be civilized before we are fit to participate in society. *Miss Manners (Judith Martin)*

54

Cats are smarter than dogs. You can't get eight cats to pull a sled through snow. *Jeff Valdez*

Dogs come when they're called; cats take a message and get back to you.   *Mary Bly*

If a cat spoke, it would say things like "Hey, I don't see the *problem* here."   *Roy Blount, Jr.*

A man who was loved by 300 women singled me out to live with him. Why? I was the only one without a cat.
Elayne Boosler

I take my pet lion to church every Sunday. He has to eat.
Marty Pollio

Cute rots the intellect.   *Garfield (Jim Davis)*

Distrust any enterprise that requires new clothes.
Henry David Thoreau (1817–1862)

61

Fashions are induced epidemics.
George Bernard Shaw (1856–1950)

62

You'd be surprised how much it costs to look this cheap.
Dolly Parton

63

There is a new awareness of style in the Soviet Union. The premier's wife recently appeared on the cover of *House and Tractor.* *Johnny Carson*

64

I should warn you that underneath these clothes I'm wearing boxer shorts and I know how to use them.
Robert Orben

65

What you have when everyone wears the same play-clothes for all occasions, is addressed by nickname, expected to participate in Show and Tell, and bullied out of any desire for privacy, is not democracy; it is kindergarten. *Miss Manners (Judith Martin)*

Being named as one of the world's best-dressed men doesn't necessarily mean that I am a bad person.

Anthony R. Cucci,
Mayor of Jersey City

67

In love there are two evils: war and peace.

Horace (65–8 B.C.)

68

Love is the crocodile on the river of desire.

Bhartrihari (ca. 625)

69

Love is what happens to men and women who don't know each other.

W. Somerset Maugham (1874–1965)

70

Love is blond. *Herbert Gold's mother*

71

The trouble with loving is that pets don't last long enough and people last too long. *Unknown*

72

A man always remembers his first love with special tenderness, but after that he begins to bunch them.

H.L. Mencken (1880–1956)

When you are in love with someone you want to be near
him all the time, except when you are out buying things
and charging them to him.

> *Miss Piggy, according to Henry Beard,*
> Miss Piggy's Guide to Life, *1981*

Better to have loved and lost a short person than never
to have loved a tall.   *David Chambless*

One of the advantages of living alone is that you don't
have to wake up in the arms of a loved one.

> *Marion Smith*

Dear Sweetheart:
> Last night I thought of you.
> At least I think it was you.
> *Love letter by Snoopy (Charles Schulz)*

In the race for love, I was scratched.
> *Joan Davis (1912–1961)*

78

Outside every thin woman is a fat man trying to get in.
Katherine Whitehorn

79

Sex is natural, but not if it's done right.   *Unknown*

80

Sex is good, but not as good as fresh sweet corn.
Garrison Keillor

81

There is hardly anyone whose sexual life, if it were broadcast, would not fill the world at large with surprise and horror.   *W. Somerset Maugham (1874–1965)*

There is nothing a young man can get by wenching but duels, the clap, and bastards.   *Kathleen Winsor*

It is more fun contemplating somebody else's navel than your own.   *Arthur Hoppe*

Of all the sexual aberrations, perhaps the most peculiar is chastity.   *Remy de Gourmont (1858–1915)*

We may eventually come to realize that chastity is no more a virtue than malnutrition.   *Alex Comfort*

I used to be a virgin, but I gave it up because there was no money in it.   *Marsha Warfield*

A terrible thing happened again last night—nothing.
                                        Phyllis Diller

88

Celibacy is not hereditary. *Guy Goden*

89

Kissing is a means of getting two people so close together that they can't see anything wrong with each other. *René Yasenek*

Oh, what lies there are in kisses!
Heinrich Heine (1797–1856)

Whenever I'm caught between two evils, I take the one I've never tried.   *Mae West (1892–1980)*

It is better to copulate than never.   *Robert Heinlein*

Vasectomy means never having to say you're sorry.
Unknown

Last night I discovered a new form of oral contraceptive. I asked a girl to go to bed with me and she said no.
Woody Allen

I told my girl friend that unless she expressed her feelings and told me what she liked I wouldn't be able to please her, so she said, "Get off me."
Garry Shandling

She was so wild that when she made French toast she got her tongue caught in the toaster.

Rodney Dangerfield

I'm too shy to express my sexual needs except over the phone to people I don't know.   *Garry Shandling*

Sex Appeal—Give Generously   *Bumper sticker*

How did sex come to be thought of as dirty in the first place? God must have been a Republican.   *Will Durst*

Before we make love, my husband takes a pain killer.

Joan Rivers

My wife was in labor with our first child for thirty-two hours and I was faithful to her the whole time.

Jonathan Katz

My wife has cut our lovemaking down to once a month,
but I know two guys she's cut out entirely.

Rodney Dangerfield

103

Chains required, whips optional.

California highway sign

104

The fantasy of every Australian man is to have two
women—one cleaning and the other dusting.

Maureen Murphy

Ouch! You're on My Hair!

Sex manual title suggested by
Richard Lewis

The difference between pornography and erotica is light-ing.   *Gloria Leonard*

If homosexuality were normal, God would have created Adam and Bruce.   *Anita Bryant*

Rub-a-dub-dub
Three men in a tub
And that's on a slow night.

Sign in a San Francisco bath house

Never play leapfrog with a unicorn.   *Unknown*

Get in good physical condition before submitting to bondage. You should be fit to be tied.   *Robert Byrne*

I caused my husband's heart attack. In the middle of lovemaking I took the paper bag off my head. He dropped the Polaroid and keeled over and so did the hooker. It would have taken me half an hour to untie myself and call the paramedics, but fortunately the Great Dane could dial. *Joan Rivers*

A British mother's advice to her daughter on how to survive the wedding night: "Close your eyes and think of England." *Pierre Daninos*

I have so little sex appeal that my gynecologist calls me "sir." *Joan Rivers*

What men call gallantry and gods adultery
Is much more common where the climate's sultry.
Lord Byron (1788–1824)

Of all the tame beasts, I hate sluts.
John Ray (1627?–1705)

I'd like to have a girl, and I'm saving my money so I can get a good one. *Bob Nickman*

117

A relationship is what happens between two people who are waiting for something better to come along.

Unknown

118

I have such poor vision I can date anybody.

Garry Shandling

119

It's relaxing to go out with my ex-wife because sne already knows I'm an idiot. *Warren Thomas*

120

I used to go out exclusively with actresses and other female impersonators. *Mort Sahl*

121

The trouble with living in sin is the shortage of closet space. *Missy Dizick*

122

The fickleness of the women I love is only equalled by the infernal constancy of the women who love me.

George Bernard Shaw (1856–1950)

123

Burt Reynolds once asked me out. I was in his room.
Phyllis Diller

124

He's the kind of man a woman would have to marry to get rid of. *Mae West (1892–1980)*

125

Brains are an asset, if you hide them.
Mae West (1892–1980)

126

He promised me earrings, but he only pierced my ears.

Arabian saying

127

Marriage is a necessary evil.

Menander (342?–291? B.C.)

128

Marriage is the only war in which you sleep with the enemy. *Unknown*

129

Nothing anybody tells you about marriage helps.

Max Siegel

130

There is so little difference between husbands you might as well keep the first.   *Adela Rogers St. Johns*

131

Marriage is really tough because you have to deal with feelings and lawyers.   *Richard Pryor*

132

Marriage could catch on again because living together is not quite living and not quite together. Premarital sex slowly evolves into premarital sox.   *Gerald Nachman*

133

Marriage is part of a sort of 50's revival package that's back in vogue along with neckties and naked ambition.
Calvin Trillin

134

I'll have to marry a virgin. I can't stand criticism.
From the movie Out of Africa, *1985*

If you are living with a man, you don't have to worry about whether you should sleep with him after dinner.

Stephanie Brush

I'd like to get married because I like the idea of a man being required by law to sleep with me every night.

Carrie Snow

Alimony is like buying oats for a dead horse.

Arthur Baer (1896–1975)

I hated my marriage, but I always had a great place to park. *Gerald Nachman*

Where I come from, when a Catholic marries a Lutheran it is considered the first step on the road to Minneapolis.

Garrison Keillor

140

I was married by a judge. I should have asked for a jury.

George Burns

141

I wouldn't trust my husband with a young woman for five minutes, and he's been dead for 25 years.

Brendan Behan's mother

142

I want a girl just like the girl that married dear old Dad.

Lyrics by Oedipus Rex

143

Adultery is a meanness and a stealing, a taking away from someone what should be theirs, a great selfishness, and surrounded and guarded by lies lest it should be found out. And out of the meanness and selfishness and lying flow love and joy and peace beyond anything that can be imagined. *Dame Rose Macaulay (1881–1958)*

144

I am a marvelous housekeeper. Every time I leave a man I keep his house. *Zsa Zsa Gabor*

The happiest time in any man's life is just after the first divorce. *John Kenneth Galbraith*

One reason people get divorced is that they run out of gift ideas. *Robert Byrne*

I've married a few people I shouldn't have, but haven't we all? *Mamie Van Doren*

What I like about masturbation is that you don't have to talk afterwards. *Milos Forman*

If sex is so personal, why do we have to share it with someone? *Unknown*

Enjoy yourself. If you can't enjoy yourself, enjoy somebody else. *Jack Schaefer*

151

The only reason I feel guilty about masturbation is that I do it so badly. *David Steinberg*

152

Philip Roth is a good writer, but I wouldn't want to
shake hands with him.

Jacqueline Susann (1921–1974)
after reading Portnoy's Complaint

153

I can't believe I forgot to have children.   *Unknown*

154

If God wanted sex to be fun, He wouldn't have included
children as punishment.   *Ed Bluestone*

I am determined my children shall be brought up in their father's religion, if they can find out what it is.

Charles Lamb (1775–1834)

I could now afford all the things I never had as a kid, if I didn't have kids.   *Robert Orben*

My mother had a great deal of trouble with me, but I think she enjoyed it.   *Mark Twain (1835–1910)*

I'll probably never have children because I don't believe in touching people for any reason.   *Paula Poundstone*

I take my children everywhere, but they always find their way back home.   *Robert Orben*

My parents put a live teddy bear in my crib.

Woody Allen

I phoned my dad to tell him I had stopped smoking. He called me a quitter.   *Steven Pearl*

Never lend your car to anyone to whom you have given birth.   *Erma Bombeck*

The best revenge is to live long enough to be a problem to your children.   *Unknown*

Children today are tyrants. They contradict their parents, gobble their food, and tyrannize their teachers.

Socrates (470–399 B.C.)

An ugly baby is a very nasty object, and the prettiest is frightful when undressed.

Queen Victoria (1819–1901)

What is more enchanting than the voices of young people when you can't hear what they say?
Logan Pearsall Smith (1865–1946)

At my lemonade stand I used to give the first glass away free and charge five dollars for the second glass. The refill contained the antidote.   *Emo Philips*

When you are eight years old, nothing is any of your business.   *Lenny Bruce (1926–1955)*

What is youth except a man or woman before it is fit to be seen?   *Evelyn Waugh (1903–1966)*

My eleven-year-old daughter mopes around the house all day waiting for her breasts to grow.   *Bill Cosby*

If you're not beguiling by age twelve, forget it.
Lucy (Charles Schulz)

172

I was so naive as a kid I used to sneak behind the barn and do nothing.   *Johnny Carson*

173

My schoolmates would make love to anything that moved, but I never saw any reason to limit myself.
Emo Philips

174

I almost got a girl pregnant in high school. It's costing me a fortune to keep the rabbit on a life-support system.
Will Shriner

175

The trouble with the 1980's as compared with the 1970's is that teenagers no longer rebel and leave home.
Marion Smith

176

Learning to dislike children at an early age saves a lot of expense and aggravation later in life.   *Robert Byrne*

177

Adolescence is the stage between infancy and adultery.
Unknown

178

I like work; it fascinates me. I can sit and look at it for hours.   *Jerome K. Jerome (1859–1927)*

179

Work is for cowards.   *Pool hustler U.J. Puckett in 1984 at age seventy-six*

180

Always be smarter than the people who hire you.
Lena Horne

181

The trouble with unemployment is that the minute you wake up in the morning you're on the job.
Slappy White

182

The volume of paper expands to fill the available brief-cases.   *Jerry Brown*

183

Any new venture goes through the following stages: enthusiasm, complication, disillusionment, search for the guilty, punishment of the innocent, and decoration of those who did nothing.   *Unknown*

When I realized that what I had turned out to be was a lousy, two-bit pool hustler and drunk, I wasn't depressed at all. I was glad to have a profession.

Danny McGoorty (1901–1970)

The reason American cities are prosperous is that there is no place to sit down.   *Alfred J. Talley*

Gardner's Law: Eighty-seven percent of all people in all professions are incompetent.   *John Gardner*

It is time I stepped aside for a less experienced and less able man.   *Professor Scott Elledge*
on his retirement from Cornell

The only way to succeed is to make people hate you.

Josef von Sternberg (1894–1969)

189

A man can't get rich if he takes proper care of his family.
Navajo saying

190

I believe that the power to make money is a gift from
God.   *John D. Rockefeller (1839–1937)*

191

It is the wretchedness of being rich that you have to live
with rich people.   *Logan Pearsall Smith (1865–1946)*

192

Never invest in anything that eats or needs repairing.
Billy Rose (1899–1966)

193

Every morning I get up and look through the Forbes list
of the richest people in America. If I'm not there, I go to
work.   *Robert Orben*

194

I enjoy being a highly overpaid actor.   *Roger Moore*

Buy old masters. They bring better prices than young mistresses. *Lord Beaverbrook (1879–1964)*

The income tax has made liars out of more Americans than golf. *Will Rogers (1879–1935)*

Why is there so much month left at the end of the money? *Unknown*

Today you can go to a gas station and find the cash register open and the toilets locked. They must think toilet paper is worth more than money. *Joey Bishop*

Enjoy money while you have it. Shrouds don't have pockets. *Virginia Esberg's grandmother*

It is no disgrace to be poor, but it might as well be.
Jim Grue

201

So he's short . . . he can stand on his wallet.

Jewish mother

202

Business is a good game—lots of competition and a minimum of rules. You keep score with money.

Atari founder Nolan Bushnell

203

Economists are people who work with numbers but who don't have the personality to be accountants.   *Unknown*

204

An economist's guess is liable to be as good as anybody else's.   *Will Rogers (1879–1935)*

205

Mathematics has given economics rigor, but alas, also mortis.   *Robert Heilbroner*

206

Organized crime in America takes in over forty billion dollars a year and spends very little on office supplies.

Woody Allen

207

Getting caught is the mother of invention.

Robert Byrne

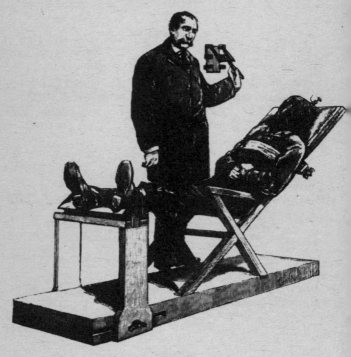

208

Capital punishment is either an affront to humanity or a potential parking place.   *Larry Brown*

I believe that people would be alive today if there were a death penalty.   *Nancy Reagan*

There is never enough time, unless you're serving it.
Malcolm Forbes

At age fifty, every man has the face he deserves.
George Orwell (1903–1950)

The secret of staying young is to live honestly, eat slowly, and lie about your age.   *Lucille Ball*

I am in the prime of senility.
Joel Chandler Harris (1848–1908)
at age fifty-eight

I am not young enough to know everything.
Oscar Wilde (1854–1900)

The closing years of life are like the end of a masquerade party, when the masks are dropped.
Arthur Schopenhauer (1788–1860)

Old age is not for sissies.   *Variously ascribed*

Old age is when the liver spots show through your gloves.   *Phyllis Diller*

Old age is like a plane flying through a storm. Once you are aboard there is nothing you can do.
Golda Meir (1898–1978)

219

When I was young there was no respect for the young, and now that I am old there is no respect for the old. I missed out coming and going.

J.B. Priestley (1894—1984)

220

Middle age begins with the first mortgage and ends when you drop dead. *Herb Caen*

221

You know you're old when you notice how young the derelicts are getting. *Jeanne Phillips*

222

My grandfather used to make home movies and edit out the joy. *Richard Lewis*

223

I smoke cigars because at my age if I don't have something to hang onto I might fall down. *George Burns*

224

The hardest years in life are those between ten and seventy. *Helen Hayes at age eighty-three*

After age seventy it's patch, patch, patch.

Jimmy Stewart

You have to be an antique to appreciate them.

Fay Madigan Lange

227

Death is just a distant rumor to the young. *Andy Rooney*

228

They say such nice things about people at their funerals that it makes me sad to realize that I'm going to miss mine by just a few days. *Garrison Keillor*

229

Big deal! I'm used to dust.

Gravestone epitaph requested
by Erma Bombeck

230

There is no reason for me to die. I already died in Altoona. *George Burns*

231

I know a man who gave up smoking, drinking, sex, and rich food. He was healthy right up to the time he killed himself. *Johnny Carson*

232

The only thing wrong with immortality is that it tends to go on forever. *Herb Caen*

233

There will be sex after death; we just won't be able to feel it. *Lily Tomlin*

234

Dying ought to be done in black and white. It is simply not a colorful activity. *Russell Baker*

What Einstein was to physics, what Babe Ruth was to home runs, what Emily Post was to table manners... that's what Edward G. Robinson was to dying like a dirty rat.   *Russell Baker*

PART TWO

Cynicism
Happiness
Morality
Bores
Food
Doctors
Parties
Alcohol
Music
Sports
Art
Law
Travel
Airplanes
Science
War
Movies
Politics
Presidents
Writers
and various odds and ends

236

Idealism is what precedes experience; cynicism is what follows. *David T. Wolf*

237

The cynics are right nine times out of ten.
H. L. Mencken (1880–1956)

308

No matter how cynical you get, it is impossible to keep up. *Lily Tomlin*

239

When there are two conflicting versions of a story, the wise course is to believe the one in which people appear at their worst. *H. Allen Smith (1906–1976)*

240

Half the people in America are faking it.

Robert Mitchum

241

Ignorance is the mother of admiration.

George Chapman (1599?–1634)

242

I was going to buy a copy of *The Power of Positive Thinking*, and then I thought: What the hell good would that do?   *Ronnie Shakes*

243

Nothing matters very much, and few things matter all.

Arthur Balfour (1848–1930)

244

Doing a thing well is often a waste of time.

Robert Byrne

245

Happiness is a Chinese meal; sorrow is a nourishment forever.   *Carolyn Kizer*

246

There is no happiness; there are only moments of happiness.   *Spanish proverb*

247

I am a kind of paranoiac in reverse. I suspect people of plotting to make me happy.   *J.D. Salinger*

248

Happiness is having a large, loving, caring, close-knit family in another city.   *George Burns*

249

O Lord, help me to be pure, but not yet.
St. Augustine (354–430)

250

An evil mind is a constant solace.   *Unknown*

251

A thing worth having is a thing worth cheating for.
                        W.C. Fields (1880–1946)

252

He without benefit of scruples
His fun and money soon quadruples.
                        Ogden Nash (1902–1971)

253

Living with a conscience is like driving a car with the brakes on.   *Budd Schulberg*

254

In order to preserve your self-respect, it is sometimes necessary to lie and cheat.   *Robert Byrne*

It has been my experience that folks who have no vices have very few virtues.   *Abraham Lincoln (1809–1865)*

The price of purity is purists.   *Calvin Trillin*

A bore is someone who, when you ask him how he is, tells you.   *Variously ascribed*

Some people stay longer in an hour than others do in a month.   *Howells (1837–1920)*

There are very few people who don't become more interesting when they stop talking.   *Mary Lowry*

The opposite of talking isn't listening. The opposite of talking is waiting. *Fran Lebowitz*

When the Emperor Constantine turned Christian, he banned the eating of sausage, which of course immediately created a whole army of sausage bootleggers and may explain why Al Capone always looked like a sausage. *Donald E. Westlake*

A louse in the cabbage is better than no meat at all.
Pennsylvania Dutch proverb

The food in Yugoslavia is fine if you like pork tartare.
Ed Begley, Jr.

Eating an artichoke is like getting to know someone really well. *Willi Hastings*

I will not eat oysters. I want my food dead—not sick, not wounded—dead. *Woody Allen*

Only Irish coffee provides in a single glass all four essential food groups: alcohol, caffeine, sugar, and fat.
Alex Levine

Cogito ergo dim sum. *(Therefore I think these are pork buns.)* *Robert Byrne*

Anybody who doesn't think that the best hamburger place in the world is in his home town is a sissy.
Calvin Trillin

You can find your way across the country using burger joints the way a navigator uses stars. *Charles Kuralt*

Part of the secret of success in life is to eat what you like and let the food fight it out inside.

Mark Twain (1835–1910)

We didn't starve, but we didn't eat chicken unless we were sick, or the chicken was.

Bernard Malamud (1914–1986)

In Mexico we have a word for sushi: bait. *José Simon*

Everything you see I owe to spaghetti. *Sophia Loren*

Blow in its ear.

*Johnny Carson on the best way
to thaw a frozen turkey*

If you want to look young and thin, hang around old fat people. *Jim Eason*

The cherry tomato is a marvelous invention, producing as it does a satisfactorily explosive squish when bitten.
Miss Manners (Judith Martin)

I prefer Hostess fruit pies to pop-up toaster tarts because they don't require so much cooking. *Carrie Snow*

You are where you eat. *Unknown*

No diet will remove all the fat from your body because the brain is entirely fat. Without a brain you might look good, but all you could do is run for public office.
Covert Bailey

280

I can get along with anybody . . . provided they're fat.
Susan Richman

281

Anybody who believes that the way to a man's heart is through his stomach flunked geography.   *Robert Byrne*

282

The waist is a terrible thing to mind.
Ziggy (Tom Wilson)

283

I have learned to spell hors d'oeuvres,
Which grates on many people's nerves.   *Unknown*

284

The trouble with eating Italian food is that five or six days later you're hungry again.   *George Miller*

285

There is no love sincerer than the love of food.
George Bernard Shaw (1856–1950)

286

Statistics show that of those who contract the habit of eating, very few survive. *Wallace Irwin (1875–1959)*

287

Marriage is not merely sharing the fettucini, but sharing the burden of finding the fettucini restaurant in the first place. *Calvin Trillin*

288

My wife and I tried to breakfast together, but we had to stop or our marriage would have been wrecked.
Winston Churchill (1874–1965)

My doctor gave me two weeks to live. I hope they're in August. *Ronnie Shakes*

The trouble with heart disease is that the first symptom is often hard to deal with: sudden death.
Michael Phelps, M.D.

One of my problems is that I internalize everything. I can't express anger; I grow a tumor instead.
Woody Allen

A male gynecologist is like an auto mechanic who has never owned a car. *Carrie Snow*

After a year in therapy, my psychiatrist said to me, "Maybe life isn't for everyone." *Larry Brown*

294

Half of analysis is anal.   *Marty Indik*

295

Why should I tolerate a perfect stranger at the bedside of my mind?   *Vladimir Nabokov (1899–1977)*
on psychoanalysis

296

People who say you're just as old as you feel are all wrong, fortunately.   *Russell Baker*

297

To reduce stress, avoid excitement. Spend more time with your spouse.   *Robert Orben*

298

Nancy Reagan has agreed to be the first artificial heart donor.   *Andrea C. Michaels*

299

Be true to your teeth or your teeth will be false to you.
Dental proverb

300

You're ugly. Not only that, you need a root canal.
James J. Garrett, D.D.S.

301

Attention to health is life's greatest hindrance.
Plato (427?—347 B.C.)

Plato was a bore.   *Friedrich Nietzsche (1844–1900)*

Nietzsche was stupid and abnormal.
                              Leo Tolstoy (1828–1910)

302
Never give a party if you will be the most interesting person there.   *Mickey Friedman*

303
Support wildlife. Throw a party.   *Unknown*

304
Cockroaches and socialites are the only things that can stay up all night and eat anything.   *Herb Caen*

305
Never mistake endurance for hospitality.   *Unknown*

306

Nothing spoils a good party like a genius.
Elsa Maxwell (1883–1963)

307

For a single woman, preparing for company means wiping the lipstick off the milk carton.   *Elayne Boosler*

308

In America, you can always find a party. In Russia, the party always finds you.   *Yakov Smirnoff*

309

The best thing about a cocktail party is being asked to it.
Gerald Nachman

310

There is nothing for a case of nerves like a case of beer.
Joan Goldstein

311

Reminds me of my safari in Africa. Somebody forgot the corkscrew and for several days we had to live on nothing but food and water. *W.C. Fields (1880–1946)*

312

Sometimes too much to drink is barely enough.
Mark Twain (1835–1910)

313

Like a camel, I can go without a drink for seven days—
and have on several horrible occasions.   *Herb Caen*

314

My grandmother is over eighty and still doesn't need glasses. Drinks right out of the bottle. *Henny Youngman*

315

There is no law against composing music when one has no ideas whatsoever. The music of Wagner, therefore, is perfectly legal. *The* National, *Paris, 1850*

316

The prelude to *Tristan and Isolde* sounded as if a bomb had fallen into a large music factory and had thrown all the notes into confusion. *The* Tribune, *Berlin, 1871*

317

The prelude to *Tristan and Isolde* reminds me of the Italian painting of the martyr whose intestines are slowly being unwound from his body on a reel.

Eduard Hanslick (1825–1904), 1868

318

Wagner drives the nail into your head with swinging hammer blows.

P.A. Fiorentino (1806–1864), Paris, 1867

9W.
Answer to the question: Do you spell your name with a V, Mr. Vagner? *Steve Allen*

320

A gentleman is a man who can play the accordion but doesn't. *Unknown*

321

There are some experiences in life which should not be demanded twice from any man, and one of them is listening to the Brahms *Requiem*.
George Bernard Shaw (1856–1950)

322

Classical music is music written by famous dead foreigners. *Arlene Heath*

323

The main thing the public demands of a composer is that he be dead. *Arthur Honegger (1892–1955)*

324

Do it big or stay in bed.

Opera producer Larry Kelly

325

Assassins!

Arturo Toscanini (1867–1957) to his orchestra

I only know two pieces—one is *Clair de Lune* and the other one isn't. *Victor Borge*

Elvis Presley had nothing to do with excellence, just myth. *Marlon Brando*

Anybody who has listened to certain kinds of music, or read certain kinds of poetry, or heard certain kinds of performances on the concertina, will admit that even suicide has its brighter aspects.

Stephen Leacock (1869—1944)

329

MTV is the lava lamp of the 1980's.   *Doug Ferrari*

330

When I was young we didn't have MTV; we had to take drugs and go to concerts.   *Steven Pearl*

331

Music is essentially useless, as life is.

George Santayana (1863—1952)

332

Show me a good loser and I'll show you a loser.

Unknown

333

Show me a good loser and I'll show you an idiot.

Leo Durocher

334

Try to hate your opponent. Even if you are playing your grandmother, try to beat her fifty to nothing. If she already has three, try to beat her fifty to three.

Danny McGoorty (1901–1969),
billiard player

335

I probably couldn't play for me. I wouldn't like my attitude.   *John Thompson, Georgetown basketball coach*

336

A team should be an extension of the coach's personality. My teams were arrogant and obnoxious.

Al McGuire, former basketball coach

337

My toughest fight was with my first wife.

Muhammad Ali

338

Hurting people is my business.   *Sugar Ray Robinson*

339

Football players, like prostitutes, are in the business of ruining their bodies for the pleasure of strangers.
Merle Kessler

340

I'm no different from anybody else with two arms, two legs, and forty-two-hundred hits. *Pete Rose*

341

Any pitcher who throws at a batter and deliberately tries to hit him is a communist.

Alvin Dark, former baseball coach

The highlight of my baseball career came in Philadelphia's Connie Mack Stadium when I saw a fan fall out of the upper deck. When he got up and walked away the crowd booed.   *Bob Uecker*

One night we play like King Kong, the next night like Fay Wray.   *Terry Kennedy, catcher for the*
                                          San Diego Padres

If I ever needed a brain transplant, I'd choose a sportswriter because I'd want a brain that had never been used.   *Norm Van Brocklin (1926–1983)*

Stuffed deer heads on walls are bad enough, but it's worse when they are wearing dark glasses and have streamers and ornaments in their antlers because then you know they were enjoying themselves at a party when they were shot.

Ellen DeGeneris

346

Golf is a game with the soul of a 1956 Rotarian.

Bill Mandel

347

Golf is the most fun you can have without taking your clothes off.   *Chi Chi Rodríguez*

348

If Borg's parents hadn't liked the name, he might never have been Bjorn.   *Murty Indik*

349

The Rose Bowl is the only bowl I've ever seen that I didn't have to clean.   *Erma Bombeck*

350

How could I lose to such an idiot?
> *A shout from chess grandmaster*
> *Aaron Nimzovich (1886–1935)*

351

I hate all sports as rabidly as a person who likes sports hates common sense.   *H.L. Mencken (1880–1956)*

352

Running is an unnatural act, except from enemies and to the bathroom.   *Unknown*

I believe that professional wrestling is clean and everything else in the world is fixed.   *Frank Deford*

ᴄᴬ◎ᴴ◎ᴬᴼ

354

Art, like morality, consists of drawing the line somewhere.   *G.K. Chesterton (1874–1936)*

355

These is not art to me, all these squares and things. Real art has, you know, like a madonna in it.
Unknown (from the guest book at
an exhibition of modern art)

356

I'm glad the old masters are all dead, and I only wish they had died sooner.   *Mark Twain (1835–1910)*

357

Give me a museum and I'll fill it.
Pablo Picasso (1881–1973)

358

Agree, for the law is costly.

William Camden (1551–1623)

359

It is better to be a mouse in a cat's mouth than a man in a lawyer's hands.   *Spanish proverb*

360

Two farmers each claimed to own a certain cow. While one pulled on its head and the other pulled on its tail, the cow was milked by a lawyer.   *Jewish parable*

361

Whatever their other contributions to our society, lawyers could be an important source of protein.

Guindon cartoon caption

362

Law school is the opposite of sex. Even when it's good it's lousy.   *Unknown*

How to win a case in court: If the law is on your side, pound on the law; if the facts are on your side, pound on the facts; if neither is on your side, pound on the table. *Unknown*

Injustice is relatively easy to bear; what stings is justice. *H.L. Mencken (1880–1956)*

Nobody wants justice. *Alan Dershowitz*

I'm not an ambulance chaser. I'm usually there before the ambulance. *Melvin Belli*

I never travel without my diary. One should always have something sensational to read.
Oscar Wilde (1854–1900)

The Irish are a fair people—they never speak well of one another.   *Samuel Johnson (1709–1784)*

There are still parts of Wales where the only concession to gaiety is a striped shroud.   *Gwyn Thomas*

I don't have any idea what I'm doing here. I didn't even know Alaska Airlines had a flight to Leningrad.

Bob and Ray

In Italy a woman can have a face like a train wreck if she's blonde.   *Unknown*

If you are going to America, bring food.

Fran Lebowitz

California is a great place to live if you're an orange.   *Fred Allen (1894–1956)*

In California you lose a point off your IQ every year.   *Truman Capote (1924–1984)*

Nothing is wrong with Southern California that a rise in the ocean level wouldn't cure.

Ross MacDonald (1915–1983)

There are two million interesting people in New York and only seventy-eight in Los Angeles.   *Neil Simon*

It is true that I was born in Iowa, but I can't speak for my twin sister.   *Abigail Van Buren (Dear Abby)*

Parts of Texas look like Kansas with a goiter.   *Unknown*

I have just returned from Boston. It is the only thing to do if you find yourself there.   *Fred Allen (1894–1956)*

380

Thanks to the Interstate Highway System, it is now possible to travel from coast to coast without seeing anything. *Charles Kuralt*

381

One of the first things schoolchildren in Texas learn is how to compose a simple declarative sentence without the word *shit* in it.   *Unknown*

382

The town was so dull that when the tide went out it refused to come back.   *Fred Allen (1894–1956)*

383

If you don't miss a few planes during the year you are spending too much time at airports.   *Paul C. Martin*

384

It is now possible for a flight attendant to get a pilot pregnant.   *Richard J. Ferris, president, United Airlines*

385

The odds against there being a bomb on a plane are a million to one, and against two bombs a million times a million to one. Next time you fly, cut the odds and take a bomb.   *Benny Hill*

386

If God had intended us to fly he would never have given us railways. *Michael Flanders*

There are two kinds of air travel in the United States, first class and third world.   *Bobby Slayton*

Thank God men cannot as yet fly and lay waste the sky as well as the earth!   *Henry David Thoreau (1817–1862)*

389

Art is I; science is we.　*Claude Bernard (1813–1878)*

390

Life is extinct on other planets because their scientists were more advanced than ours.　*Unknown*

391

A stitch in time would have confused Einstein.

Unknown

392

Great moments in science: Einstein discovers that time is actually money.　*Gary Larson cartoon caption*

393

Technological progress is like an axe in the hands of a pathological criminal.　*Albert Einstein (1879–1955)*

394

Technology is a way of organizing the universe so that man doesn't have to experience it. *Max Frisch*

395

Horsepower was a wonderful thing when only horses had it. *Unknown*

396

Men have become the tools of their tools.
Henry David Thoreau (1817–1862)

397

The computer is down. I hope it's something serious. *Stanton Delaplane*

398

Rivers in the United States are so polluted that acid rain makes them cleaner. *Andrew Malcolm*

A two-pound turkey and a fifty-pound cranberry—that's Thanksgiving dinner at Three-Mile Island.

Johnny Carson

The scientific theory I like best is that the rings of Saturn are composed entirely of lost airline luggage.

Mark Russell

Energy experts have announced the development of a new fuel made from human brain tissue. It's called assohol.   *George Carlin*

❧◖❀◗❧

What a beautiful fix we are in now; peace has been declared.   *Napoleon Bonaparte (1769–1821)*
                    after the Treaty of Amiens, 1802

I thoroughly disapprove of duels. If a man should challenge me, I would take him kindly and forgivingly by the hand and lead him to a quiet place and kill him.
                    Mark Twain (1835–1910)

There is nothing more exhilarating than to be shot at without result.   *Winston Churchill (1874–1965)*

Nobody ever forgets where he buried the hatchet.
                    Kin Hubbard (1868–1930)

Will the last person out of the tunnel turn out the light?   *Graffito in Saigon, 1973*

⋘◈H◈⋙

407

We are what we are.   *Motto of Lake Wobegone,*
according to Garrison Keillor

408

You gotta live somewhere.   *Motto for Cleveland*
suggested by Jimmy Brogan

400

It's a living.   *Motto for the U.S. Army*
suggested by Mort Sahl

410

What died?   *Motto for New Jersey*
suggested by Steven Pearl

411

What the hell are you looking at?

*License plate slogan for New York
suggested by Steven Pearl*

412

Eat cheese or die.

*Motto for Wisconsin
suggested by Joel McNally*

413

Not you.

*Bumper sticker in the state where the
license plate slogan is You've Got a
Friend in Pennsylvania*

414

You appeal to a small, select group of confused people.

Message in fortune cookie

415

Ignore previous cookie.   *Message in fortune cookie*

You make God sick.

Message in fortune cookie
received by Rick Reynolds

❧⊙❧⊙❧

417

There is nothing wrong with Hollywood that six first-class funerals wouldn't solve.   *Unknown*

418

The length of a film should be directly related to the endurance of the human bladder.

Alfred Hitchcock (1899–1980)

419

A team effort is a lot of people doing what I say.

Michael Winner, British film director

420

You just gotta save Christianity, Richard! You gotta!

Loretta Young to Richard the Lionhearted
in the movie The Crusades, *1935*

Yer beautiful in yer wrath! I shall keep you, and in responding to my passions, yer hatred will kindle into love.
John Wayne as Genghis Khan to Susan
Hayward in the movie The Conqueror, *1956*

I've met a lot of hard-boiled eggs in my time, but you—you're twenty minutes!
From the movie Ace in the Hole, *1951*

When Elizabeth Taylor meets a man she takes him and squeezes the life out of him and then throws away the pulp. *Eddie Fisher's mother*

Elsa Lanchester looks as though butter wouldn't melt in her mouth, or anywhere else. *Maureen O'Hara*

They used to photograph Shirley Temple through gauze. They should photograph me through linoleum.
Tallulah Bankhead (1903–1968)

426

Clark Gable's ears make him look like a taxicab with the doors open.   *Howard Hughes (1905–1976)*

427

I saw the sequel to the movie *Clones*, and you know what? It was the same movie!   *Jim Samuels*

428

If you get to be a really big headliner, you have to be prepared for people throwing bottles at you in the night.
Mick Jagger

429

You have to have a talent for having talent.
Ruth Gordon (1897–1985)

430

Now that I'm over sixty I'm veering toward respectability.   *Shelley Winters*

431

A starlet is any woman under thirty not actively employed in a brothel.   *Unknown*

The human race is faced with a cruel choice: work or daytime television.   *Unknown*

Television is democracy at its ugliest.
Paddy Chayevsky (1923–1982)

Television enables you to be entertained in your home by people you wouldn't have in your home.   *David Frost*

Imitation is the sincerest form of television.
Fred Allen (1894–1956)

Never miss a chance to have sex or appear on television.
Gore Vidal

The cable TV sex channels don't expand our horizons, don't make us better people, and don't come in clearly enough.   *Bill Maher*

Babies on television never spit up on the Ultrasuede.
Erma Bombeck

Men and nations behave wisely once they have exhausted all the other alternatives.   *Abba Eban*

What luck for rulers that men do not think.
Adolf Hitler (1889–1945)

Every government is run by liars and nothing they say should be believed.   *I.F. Stone*

It is dangerous to be right when the government is wrong.   *Voltaire (1694–1778)*

Patriotism is the veneration of real estate above principles.   *George Jean Nathan (1882–1958)*

Patriotism is a pernicious, psychopathic form of idiocy.
George Bernard Shaw (1856–1950)

There is but one way for a newspaperman to look at a politician and that is down.
Frank H. Simonds (1878–1936)

Don't burn the flag; wash it.
Norman Thomas (1884–1968)

The reason there are so few female politicians is that it is too much trouble to put makeup on two faces.

Maureen Murphy

Democracy is being allowed to vote for the candidate you dislike least.   *Robert Byrne*

Diplomacy is the art of saying "Nice doggie" until you can find a rock.   *Will Rogers (1879–1935)*

An honest politician is one who when he is bought will stay bought.   *Simon Cameron (1799–1889)*

A communist is a person who publicly airs his dirty Lenin.   *Jack Pomeroy*

A conservative is a man who wants the rules changed so that no one can make a pile the way he did.

Gregory Nunn

Liberals feel unworthy of their possessions. Conservatives feel they deserve everything they've stolen.

Mort Sahl

A conservative doesn't want anything to happen for the first time; a liberal feels it should happen, but not now.

Mort Sahl

Conservative, n. A statesman who is enamored of existing evils, as distinguished from the liberal, who wishes to replace them with others.

Ambrose Bierce

They dug up an ancient Chinese emperor a while back who was encased in jade. I prefer gold.

Ed Koch, mayor of New York City

Too bad the only people who know how to run the country are busy driving cabs and cutting hair.

George Burns

Those who are too smart to engage in politics are punished by being governed by those who are dumber.

Plato (427?–347 B.C.)

Plato was a bore.   *Friedrich Nietzsche (1844–1900)*

Nietzsche was stupid and abnormal.

Leo Tolstoy (1828–1910)

If the Republicans will stop telling lies about the Democrats, we will stop telling the truth about them.

Adlai Stevenson (1900–1965)

In America, anyone can become president. That's one of the risks you take.   *Adlai Stevenson (1900–1965)*

Calvin Coolidge didn't say much, and when he did he didn't say much.   *Will Rogers (1879–1935)*

I think the American public wants a solemn ass as president. And I think I'll go along with them.
Calvin Coolidge (1872–1933)

He's alive but unconscious, just like Gerald Ford.
From the movie Airplane, *1980*

Your public servants serve you right.
Adlai Stevenson (1900–1965)

It's the responsibility of the media to look at the president with a microscope, but they go too far when they use a proctoscope.   *Richard M. Nixon*

When we got into office, the thing that surprised me the most was that things were as bad as we'd been saying they were.   *John F. Kennedy (1917–1963)*

It's our fault. We should have given him better parts.
Jack Warner on hearing that Ronald Reagan
had been elected governor of California

I have left orders to be awakened at any time in case of national emergency, even if I'm in a cabinet meeting.
Joke by Ronald Reagan, current
president of the United States

Ronald Reagan is the first president to be accompanied by a Silly Statement Repair Team.   *Mark Russell*

470

I'm glad Reagan is president. Of course, I'm a professional comedian.   *Will Durst*

471

Reagan is proof that there is life after death.   *Mort Sahl*

472

There is no distinctly American criminal class—except Congress.   *Mark Twain (1835–1910)*

473

They should stop calling Reagan and Gorbachev the two most powerful men in the world. Between the two of them they couldn't bench press a hundred pounds.
Al Ordover

474

Gary Hart is just Jerry Brown without the fruit flies.
Robert Strauss

Author's Prayer:
>   Our Father, which art in heaven,
>   And has also written a book . . .

>   *Unknown*

476

The only reason for being a professional writer is that you can't help it.   *Leo Rosten*

477

In Hollywood, writers are considered only the first drafts of human beings.   *Frank Deford*

What an author likes to write most is his signature on the back of a check.   *Brendan Francis*

Very few things happen at the right time and the rest do not happen at all. The conscientious historian will correct these defects.   *Herodotus (484–425 B.C.)*

History will be kind to me for I intend to write it.
                    Winston Churchill (1874–1965)

It is a mean thief or a successful author that plunders the dead.   *Austin O'Malley (1858–1932)*

The best part of the fiction in many novels is the notice that the characters are purely imaginary.
                    Franklin P. Adams (1881–1960)

A detective digs around in the garbage of people's lives. A novelist invents people and then digs around in their garbage.   *Joe Gores*

Fiction is obliged to stick to possibilities. Truth isn't.
                                    Mark Twain (1835–1910)

Truth is shorter than fiction.   *Irving Cohen*

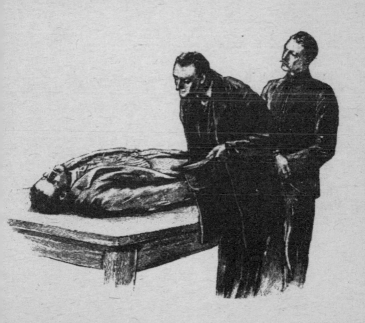

486

The only good author is a dead author.

Book editor Patrick O'Connor

487

In six pages I can't even say "hello." *James Michener*

488

Copy from one, it's plagiarism; copy from two, it's research. *Wilson Mizner (1876–1933)*

489

Originality is the art of concealing your sources.

Unknown

490

There are three rules for writing a novel. Unfortunately, no one knows what they are. *W. Somerset Maugham (1874–1965)*

Get your facts first, then you can distort them as you please.   *Mark Twain (1835–1910)*

Why don't you write books people can read?
Nora Joyce to her husband, James (1882–1941)

A Treasury of Filthy Religious Art Masterpieces.
Book once proposed to Simon & Schuster

Changing literary agents is like changing deck chairs on the *Titanic*.   *Unknown*

You can always tell book people. They are well dressed and their hair is really clean.
*Overheard by Constance Casey
at a booksellers' convention*

Teaching has ruined more American novelists than drink.
Gore Vidal

I felt like poisoning a monk.   *Umberto Eco*
on why he wrote the novel
The Name of the Rose

With the single exception of Homer, there is no eminent writer, not even Sir Walter Scott, whom I despise so entirely as I despise Shakespeare.
George Bernard Shaw (1856–1950)

I feel very old sometimes . . . I carry on and would not like to die before having emptied a few more buckets of shit on the heads of my fellow men.
Gustave Flaubert (1821–1880)

To read your own poetry in public is a kind of mental incest.   *Brendan Behan's father*

501

Nobody ever committed suicide while reading a good book, but many have while trying to write one.

Robert Byrne

502

All newspaper editorial writers ever do is come down from the hills after the battle is over and shoot the wounded. *Unknown*

503

The difference between literature and journalism is that journalism is unreadable and literature is not read.

Oscar Wilde (1854–1900)

504

Advertisements contain the only truths to be relied on in a newspaper.   *Thomas Jefferson (1743–1826)*

505

Never argue with people who buy ink by the gallon.

Tommy Lasorda

506

Some editors are failed writers, but so are most writers.

T.S. Eliot (1888–1965)

507

Every great man has his disciples, and it is always Judas who writes the biography.   *Oscar Wilde (1854–1900)*

508

Biography lends to death a new terror.

Oscar Wilde (1854–1900)

509

Autobiography is now as common as adultery and hardly less reprehensible.   *Lord Altrincham*

510

Autobiography is the last refuse of scoundrels.

Henry Gray

511

It's not a bad idea to get in the habit of writing down one's thoughts. It saves one having to bother anyone else with them.   *Isabel Colegate*

512

Book reviewers are little old ladies of both sexes.

John O'Hara (1905–1970)

Any reviewer who expresses rage and loathing for a
novel is preposterous. He or she is like a person who has
put on full armor and attacked a hot fudge sundae.

Kurt Vonnegut

People who like this sort of thing will find this the sort of
thing they like.

Book review by Abraham Lincoln (1809–1865)

A bad review is like baking a cake with all the best in-
gredients and having someone sit on it.   *Danielle Steel*

Criticism is prejudice made plausible.

H.L. Mencken (1880–1956)

Praise and criticism are both frauds.   *Unknown*

I am sitting in the smallest room in the house. I have
your review in front of me. Soon it will be behind me.
Max Reger (1873–1916)

◦⦿◦⦿◦

Quotations are a columnist's bullpen. Stealing someone
else's words frequently spares the embarrassment of eating your own.   *Peter Anderson*

It is better to be quotable than to be honest.
Tom Stoppard

This isn't much of a quote book if I'm in it.
*Richard Dowd, quoted here
for the first time anywhere*

PART THREE

Miscellaneous

522

There will be a rain dance Friday night, weather permitting.   *George Carlin*

523

Gifts are like hooks.   *Martial (40?–102?)*

524

Every time a friend succeeds, I die a little.   *Gore Vidal*

525

The goal of all inanimate objects is to resist man and ultimately defeat him.   *Russell Baker*

Cleaning anything involves making something else dirty, but anything can get dirty without something else getting clean. *Lawrence J. Peter*

You know it's not a good wax museum when there are wicks coming out of people's heads.   *Rick Reynolds*

Everything changes but the avant garde.
Paul Valéry (1871–1945)

If you can't laugh at yourself, make fun of other people.
Bobby Slayton

The world is divided into two classes—invalids and nurses. *James McNeill Whistler (1834–1903)*

Never mistake motion for action.
Ernest Hemingway (1889–1961)

Hemingway was a jerk.   *Harold Robbins*

532

I wish everybody would go back into the closet.
Josefa Heifetz

533

Some luck lies in not getting what you thought you
wanted but getting what you have, which once you have
got it you may be smart enough to see is what you would
have wanted had you known.   *Garrison Keillor*

534

All God's children are not beautiful. Most of God's children are, in fact, barely presentable.   *Fran Lebowitz*

535

Providence protects children and idiots. I know because
I have tested it.   *Mark Twain (1835–1910)*

536

The easiest kind of relationship for me is with ten thousand people. The hardest is with one.   *Joan Baez*

537

Five Kids Who Make Your Kids Look Sick
*Magazine article suggested
by Garrison Keillor*

538

I'll not listen to reason. Reason always means what
someone else has to say.
Elizabeth Cleghorn Gaskell (1810–1865)

539

Suggested magazines:

Crotch: The International Sex Weekly
Thomas Berger

Cocker Spaniel Annual Manual
Luther Vrettos

Gimme! The Magazine of Money
Robert Byrne

The Shining (Formerly Bald World)
Robert Byrne

Beautiful Spot: A Magazine of Parking
Calvin Trillin

Poor Housekeeping (ten times the circulation of Good
Housekeeping)
Robert Byrne

540

Nothing is impossible for the man who doesn't have to
do it himself. *A.H. Weiler*

541

A censor is a man who knows more than he thinks you ought to.   *Granville Hicks (1901–1982)*

542

A committee is a cul-de-sac down which ideas are lured and then quietly strangled.   *Sir Barnett Cocks (ca. 1907)*

543

As scarce as truth is, the supply has always been in excess of the demand.   *Josh Billings (1818–1885)*

544

I never forget a face, but in your case I'll be glad to make an exception. *Groucho Marx (1895–1977)*

545

I can mend the break of day, heal a broken heart, and provide temporary relief to nymphomaniacs. *Larry Lee*

546

Hell is paved with Good Samaritans.

William M. Holden

547

Enough.
Definition of "Once."

Ambrose Bierce (1842–1914?)

548

Anybody who thinks of going to bed before 12 o'clock is a scoundrel. *Samuel Johnson (1709–1784)*

A fanatic is a man who does what he thinks the Lord would do if He knew the facts of the case.

Finley Peter Dunne (1867–1936)

All movements go too far.

Bertrand Russell (1872–1970)

Never engage in a battle of wits with an unarmed person. *Unknown*

Flies spread disease—keep yours zipped. *Unknown*

Ya gotta do what ya gotta do.

Sylvester Stallone in the movie Rocky IV, *1985*

There is one thing to be said for country clubs; they drain off a lot of people you wouldn't want to associate with anyway. *Joseph Prescott*

555

I do not want people to be agreeable, as it saves me the trouble of liking them. *Jane Austen (1775–1817)*

556

A friend in need is a friend to dodge. *Unknown*

Analyzing humor is like dissecting a frog. Few people are interested and the frog dies of it.

E.B. White (1899–1985)

A lot of people like snow. I find it to be an unnecessary freezing of water.   *Carl Reiner*

I've only met four perfect people in my life and I didn't like any of them.   *Unknown*

I dote on his very absence.

William Shakespeare (1564–1616)

Shakespeare is crude, immoral, vulgar, and senseless.   *Leo Tolstoy (1828–1910)*

Often it does seem a pity that Noah and his party did not miss the boat.   *Mark Twain (1835–1910)*

562

You can't depend on your eyes when your imagination is out of focus.   *Mark Twain (1835–1910)*

563

Only dead fish swim with the stream.   *Unknown*

564

I wish people wouldn't say, "Excuse me," when I *want* them to step on my feet.   *Karen Elizabeth Gordon*

565

Either I've been missing something or nothing has been going on.   *Karen Elizabeth Gordon*

566

There are 350 varieties of shark, not counting loan and pool.   *L.M. Boyd*

567

When in doubt, duck.   *Malcolm Forbes*

American college students are like American colleges—
each has half-dulled faculties.
James Thurber (1894–1961)

It took me twenty years of studied self-restraint, aided
by the natural decay of my faculties, to make myself dull
enough to be accepted as a serious person by the British
public.   *George Bernard Shaw (1856–1950)*

The longer I live the more I see that I am never wrong
about anything, and that all the pains I have so humbly
taken to verify my notions have only wasted my time.
George Bernard Shaw (1856–1950)

I don't care what you ♥.   *Bumper sticker*

I ♠ my pets.   *Bumper sticker*

573

Love your enemies in case your friends turn out to be a bunch of bastards.   *R.A. Dickson*

574

One should forgive one's enemies, but not before they are hanged.   *Heinrich Heine (1797–1856)*

575

Experience teaches you to recognize a mistake when you've made it again.   *Unknown*

576

Good judgment comes from experience, and experience comes from bad judgment.   *Barry LePatner*

577

The trouble with using experience as a guide is that the final exam often comes first and then the lesson.

Unknown

578

It's not what we don't know that hurts, it's what we know that ain't so.   *Will Rogers (1879–1935)*

579

The world is a madhouse, so it's only right that it is patrolled by armed idiots. *Brendan Behan*

580

Consistency requires you to be as ignorant today as you were a year ago. *Bernard Berenson (1865–1959)*

581

Correct me if I'm wrong, but hasn't the fine line between sanity and madness gotten finer? *George Price*

582

The reason lightning doesn't strike twice in the same place is that the same place isn't there the second time. *Willie Tyler*

583

The nail that sticks up gets hammered down.

Japanese proverb

584

You can lead a horse to water, but you can't make him float. *Unknown*

585

If you want a place in the sun, prepare to put up with a few blisters. *Abigail Van Buren*

I don't know, I've never been kippled.
Answer to the question: Do you like Kipling?

Unknown

Ford used to have a better idea; now they don't have a clue. *Steve Kravitz*

I can't believe that out of 100,000 sperm, you were the quickest. *Steven Pearl*

Honesty is the best image. *Ziggy (Tom Wilson)*

Silence is argument carried on by other means.
Ernesto "Che" Guevara (1928—1967)

Soderquist's Paradox:
 There are more horse's asses than horses.

From 1,001 *Logical Laws,*
compiled by John Peers

Do Not Disturb signs should be written in the language of the hotel maids.   *Tim Bedore*

What ought to be done to the man who invented the celebrating of anniversaries? Mere killing would be too light.   *Mark Twain (1835–1910)*

Status quo. Latin for the mess we're in.   *Jeve Moorman*

Never put off until tomorrow what you can do the day after tomorrow.   *Mark Twain (1835–1910)*

596

Nobody can make you feel inferior without your consent.   *Eleanor Roosevelt (1884–1962)*

597

An intellectual is a person whose mind watches itself.
Albert Camus (1913–1960)

598

The average person thinks he isn't.
Father Larry Lorenzoni

599

Sleep is an eight-hour peep show of infantile erotica.
J.G. Ballard

600

No man can think clearly when his fists are clenched.
George Jean Nathan (1882–1958)

601

Propaganda is the art of persuading others of what you don't believe yourself.   *Abba Eban*

602

Never believe anything until it has been officially denied.
Claud Cockburn (1904–1981)

603

There are only two ways of telling the complete truth—anonymously and posthumously.   *Thomas Sowell*

604

There is only one thing about which I am certain, and that is that there is very little about which one can be certain.   *W. Somerset Maugham (1874–1965)*

605

Before they made S.J. Perelman they broke the mold.
Unknown

606

Here's to our wives and sweethearts—may they never meet.   *John Bunny (1866–1939)*

607

Man Robs, Then Kills Himself.

Headline in Vancouver Province, June 21, 1978

608

Don't jump on a man unless he's down.

Finley Peter Dunne (1867–1936)

609

Just because your voice reaches halfway around the world doesn't mean you are wiser than when it reached only to the end of the bar.

Edward R. Murrow (1908–1965)

610

Glory is fleeting, but obscurity is forever.

Napoleon Bonaparte (1769–1821)

611

It is fun being in the same decade with you.

Franklin Delano Roosevelt (1882–1945) in a letter to Winston Churchill, 1942

Although prepared for martyrdom, I preferred that it be postponed.   *Winston Churchill (1874–1965)*

The higher a monkey climbs, the more you see of its behind.
   General Joseph "Vinegar Bend" Stilwell (1883–1946)

Marie Osmond makes Mother Teresa look like a slut.
   Joan Rivers

What a strange illusion it is to suppose that beauty is goodness.   *Leo Tolstoy (1828–1910)*

I'm not going to climb into the ring with Tolstoy
   Ernest Hemingway (1889–1961)

Hemingway was a jerk.   *Harold Robbins*

616

As Miss America, my goal is to bring peace to the entire world and then to get my own apartment.   *Jay Leno*

617

I hate the outdoors. To me the outdoors is where the car is.   *Will Durst*

618

The other day a dog peed on me. A bad sign.
H. L. Mencken (1880–1956)

✦❦✦

619

He grounds the warship he walks on.
*John Bracken on Captain Barney Kelly,
who ran the USS* Enterprise *into the mud of
San Francisco Bay in May of 1983*

620

These are the souls that time men's tries.

Sports Illustrated *on official timers at track meets*

621

Astrology is Taurus.   *F. W. Dedering*

622

Nobody outside of a baby carriage or a judge's chamber
believes in an unprejudiced point of view.
Lillian Hellman (1907–1984)

623

If I don't get a part for my artificial heart
I'm gonna stop caring for you.
Lyrics by Bernie Sheehan

624

I Can't Give You Anything But Love and a Baby
Song title by Willie Tyler

625

If the Phone Doesn't Ring, It's Me
Song title by Jimmy Buffet

626

It isn't that gentlemen really prefer blondes, it's just that we look dumber.   *Anita Loos (1893–1981)*

627

She was what we used to call a suicide blonde—dyed by her own hand.   *Saul Bellow*

628

For people who like peace and quiet: a phoneless cord.
Unknown

629

The best audience is intelligent, well-educated, and a little drunk.   *Alben W. Barkley (1877–1956)*

630

What is this, an audience or an oil painting?

Milton Berle

631

Civilization exists by geological consent, subject to change without notice. *Will Durant (1885–1981)*

632

In Biblical times, a man could have as many wives as he could afford. Just like today. *Abigail Van Buren*

633

The first human being who hurled an insult instead of a stone was the founder of civilization.

Attributed to Sigmund Freud (1856–1939)

634

The only paradise is paradise lost. *Marcel Proust (1871–1922)*

Historical reminder: always put Horace before Descartes. *Donald O. Rickter*

Most of our future lies ahead.
                    Denny Crum, Louisville basketball coach

If there is another way to skin a cat, I don't want to know about it. *Steve Kravitz*

Sources, References, and Notes

∽◎◦◎◦

Quotations are indexed here only when I have something useful to add. Readers with corrections or who can supply missing information are urged to write to me in care of Fawcett Books, 201 E. 50th Street, New York, New York 10022.

Quotation
Number
2. BS in a letter to RB.
3. JDM in the *Bulletin*, 1974
5. LT in *What Is Religion?*, 1902.
8. HLM in an Associated Press interview, 1941.
9. RM in *The Towers of Trebizond*, 1956.
10. Quoted by G. M. Thomson in *Vote of Censure*, 1968.
11. BM in a speech in Lausanne, 1904.
13. CK is a standup comedian.
14. From the television series "All in the Family." Thanks to George Aronek.
16. Quoted in the *San Francisco Chronicle*, December 17, 1985.
17. According to William Safire in his syndicated column, December 8, 1985.
18. FN in *Thus Spake Zarathustra*.
19. EH in a letter.
20. HR as quoted in Leslie Halliwell's *The Filmgoer's Companion*, 1984.

22. RS is a standup comedian.
25. From *The Cynic's Lexicon*, compiled by Jonathon Green, 1982.
26. Thanks to David Huard.
27. FN in *Thus Spake Zarathustra*, 1891.
28. Quoted in *3500 Good Quotes for Speakers*, compiled by Gerald F. Lieberman, 1983.
30. NW quoted in *Was It Good for You, Too?* compiled by Bob Chieger, 1983.
31. WA in *Play It Again, Sam*, 1969.
33. Quoted in the *San Francisco Sunday Chronicle-Examiner*, September 1, 1985.
35. O in *Ars Amatoria*.
36. J in *Satires*, A.D. 110.
37. From *A New Dictionary of Quotations on Historical Principles*, compiled by H. L. Mencken, 1952.
39. SR in the *San Francisco Chronicle*, August 2, 1985.
44. Taken from the jacket of MP's 1985 book *Shoes Never Lie*.
45. AC is a standup comedian.
47. Quoted in the comedy trade paper *Just for Laughs*, August 1985.
51. Quoted in *Forbes*, September 16, 1985.
53. JM in *Miss Manners' Guide to Excruciatingly Correct Behavior*, 1985.
54. JV is a standup comedian.
55. MD in *Dogs Are Better Than Cats*, 1985.
56. RB in the *Atlantic Monthly*, February 1985.
57. EB is a standup comedian.
58. MP is a standup comedian.
62. Quoted in the *San Francisco Chronicle*, December 31, 1984.
63. "The Tonight Show," January 10, 1985.
64. RO in *Orben's Current Comedy*, a weekly newsletter of topical gags, November 6, 1985.
65. JM in *Common Courtesy*, 1985.
66. ARC was interviewed by the *New York Times* in December 1985. He was quoted further as saying that he didn't rule out the possibility that the honor bestowed on him was a political smear.
68. See note 37.

70. Quoted by HG in his autobiographical novel *Family.*
72. Thanks to H. Peter Metzger.
73. From *Miss Piggy's Guide to Life*, 1981, as told to HB.
74. From *Quote*, November 1, 1985.
75. MS to RB.
76. From the Peanuts comic strip, April 1984.
78. KW is a popular columnist in Great Britain.
80. GK on his radio show "A Prairie Home Companion," July 21, 1985.
83. AH in the *San Francisco Chronicle*, November 25, 1985.
84. Quoted in *The Cynic's Lexicon*, compiled by Jonathon Green, 1982.
85. AC in the *New York Times*, February 18, 1968.
86. MW at the San Francisco Standup Comedy Competition, 1979.
88. GG in a letter to the *Journal of Irreproducible Results*.
89. RY in *Family Weekly*, 1977.
92. Thanks to Marty Indik.
95. GS is a standup comedian.
97. GS on "The Tonight Show," August 17, 1985.
98. Seen in London by Herb Caen.
99. WD won the 1983 San Francisco Standup Comedy Competition.
100. Given in *Was It Good for You, Too?* compiled by Bob Chieger, 1983.
101. JK is a standup comedian.
104. MM is a standup comedian.
105. Quoted by Peter Stack in the *San Francisco Chronicle*, October 4, 1985. RL is a standup comedian.
106. GL is publisher of *High Society*.
107. AB in *Rolling Stone*, July 14, 1977.
112. PD in his 1955 novel *Major Thompson Lives in France and Discovers the French*.
114. LB in *Don Juan*, 1819.
116. BN is a standup comedian. Thanks to Pete Harley.
117. Thanks to Lee Simon.
118. GS is a standup comedian.

119. WT is a standup comedian.
121. MD to RB.
124. From the movie *She Done Him Wrong* (1933), screenplay by MW.
129. MS in the *New York Times Book Review*, November 6, 1985.
132. GN is a columnist and critic for the *San Francisco Chronicle*.
134. *Out of Africa*, screenplay by Kurt Luedtke based on books by and about Isak Dinesen.
135. SB in *Men: An Owner's Manual*, 1984.
136. CS is a standup comedian.
138. GN in the *San Francisco Chronicle*, February 26, 1985.
139. GK in his San Francisco lecture, December 13, 1984.
141. Thanks to Susan Richman.
142. Thanks to Arlene Heath.
143. RM in *The Towers of Trebizond*, 1956.
145. Quoted in *Was It Good for You, Too?* compiled by Bob Chieger, 1983.
147. Thanks to Merla Zellerbach.
149. Thanks to Susan Richman.
150. Quoted by Herb Caen in the *San Francisco Chronicle*, December 23, 1983.
151. DS on "The Tonight Show," 1972.
156. See note 64.
158. PP is a standup comedian.
159. See note 64.
161. SP is a standup comedian.
165. In *Letter and Journals* (New York: Viking, 1985).
166. LPS in *Afterthoughts*, 1934.
167. EP is a standup comedian.
174. WS is a standup comedian.
175. MS to RB.
180. LH on "Freeman Reports," November 30, 1985.
181. Thanks to Joe Gores.
184. In RB's biography *McGoorty*, 1972 and 1984.
186. JG in *Esquire*, April 1983.
187. Thanks to Knox Burger.
191. LPS in *All Trivia*, 1949.
193. See note 64.

194. RM at a San Francisco press conference, May 21, 1985.
199. Quoted by Merla Zellerbach in the *San Francisco Chronicle*, March 7, 1984.
200. Quoted in the *Little Dublin News*, March 1985, published in Dubuque, Iowa.
208. LB in the *San Francisco Examiner*, July 15, 1984.
220. HC in the *San Francisco Chronicle*, April 28, 1985.
226. FML to RB.
228. GK in his San Francisco lecture, December 13, 1984.
231. JC on "The Tonight Show," November 20, 1984.
232. HC in the *San Francisco Chronicle*, December 11, 1985.
234–235. RB in his syndicated *New York Times* column, September 22, 1985.
236. OTW to RB.
238. LT in her one-woman Broadway show, 1985.
239. HAS in *Let the Crabgrass Grow*, 1960.
241. GC in *The Widow's Tears*, 1612.
242. RS is a standup comedian.
245. CK won the Pulitzer Prize for poetry in 1985.
246. Quoted in *Hot News*, published periodically by Lyle Stuart.
251. Thanks to David Huard.
252. Thanks to Marty Indik.
253. BS in *What Makes Sammy Run?* 1941.
256. CT in *American Fried*, 1979.
259. ML in the *Pacific Sun*, November 15, 1985.
260. FL in *Social Studies*, 1981.
261. DL in *A Likely Story*, 1984.
262. EB on "The Tonight Show," September 25, 1985.
264. Quoted by Herb Caen in the *San Francisco Chronicle*, May 6, 1985.
265. WA in *Please Don't Drink the Water*, 1967.
266. Quoted by Herb Caen in the *San Francisco Chronicle*, December 13, 1984.
268. CT in *American Fried*, 1979.
271. BM in *Idiots First*, 1963.
272. JS is a standup comedian.
275. JE is a San Francisco radio talk-show host.

277. CS is a standup comedian.
279. CB in his San Rafael, California lecture, February 1985.
283. Thanks to H. Peter Metzger.
284. GM is a standup comedian.
289. RS is a standup comedian.
290. MP on the BBC World Service.
292–293. Delivered on Comedy Celebration Day, July 20, 1985, when sixty standup comedians performed for a total of seven hours in San Francisco's Golden Gate Park.
296. RB in his syndicated *New York Times* column, August 27, 1985.
297. See note 64.
298. Quoted by Herb Caen in the *San Francisco Chronicle*, March 7, 1985.
299. Thanks to Dr. Stephen F. Goodman.
300. JJG to RB in jest; RB didn't need a root canal.
302. Thanks to Collin Wilcox.
305. Thanks to Audrey Stanley, KARN, Little Rock.
307. EB is a standup comedian.
308. YS is a Soviet comedian who emigrated to the United States in 1981. He also said that in the United States you watch television, but in Russia television watches you.
309. GN in the *San Francisco Chronicle*, August 27, 1985.
313. HC in the *San Francisco Chronicle*, December 29, 1985. The quote is out of context, for it appeared in a column in which HC argued that drunk jokes aren't really funny and vowed to use fewer of them in his widely-read column.
315–318. Many quotes of this sort can be found in *The Lexicon of Musical Invective*, compiled by Nicolas Slonimsky, 1969.
319. From the Question Man segment of the old "Steve Allen Show."
320. Thanks to Kitty Sprague.
322. AH to RB.
327. MB in *Playboy*, 1979.
328. SL in *The Mariposa Bank Mystery*, 1912.
330. SP is a standup comedian.

331. GS in *The Life of Reason*, 1954.
332. Thanks to Leonard Tong.
333. As quoted by RB in *McGoorty*, 1972 and 1984.
337. Quoted by Bob Green in *Cheeseburgers*. Thanks to Tom Winston.
338. RR to the New York State Boxing Commission, May 23, 1962.
339. Quoted by Patricia Holt in the *San Francisco Chronicle*, November 13, 1985.
341. Thanks to Marty Indik.
342. BU on "Larry King Live," September 17, 1985.
345. EG is a standup comedian.
346. BD in the *San Francisco Examiner*, February 10, 1985.
349. EB was the grand marshal of the 1986 Rose Bowl Parade.
353. FD on Cable News Network, November 4, 1985.
357. Quoted by Barnaby Conrad III in the *San Francisco Chronicle*, November 24, 1985.
362–363. Thanks to Arlene Heath.
366. Quoted in the *San Francisco Chronicle*, August 10, 1985.
369. GT in *Punch*, June 18, 1958.
370. From a sketch titled *Fern Ock Veek, Sickly Whale Oil Processor*, reprinted in *The New! Improved! Bob and Ray Book*, 1985.
371. Quoted by Stephanie von Buchau in the *Pacific Sun*, February 8, 1985.
372. FL in *Social Studies*, 1981.
373. From *Conversations with Capote*, by Lawrence Grobel.
375. RM in *The Drowning Pool*, 1951.
376. NS in *Playboy*, February 1979.
377. Letter to RB.
379. Letter to Groucho Marx, June 12, 1953.
383. Thanks to Susan Richman.
386. MF in the *New York Times*, April 16, 1975.
387. BS is a standup comedian.
388. HDT in *Journal*, January 3, 1861.
391. From *The Journal of Irreproducible Results*. Thanks to D. O. Rickter.
397. SD in the *San Francisco Chronicle*, July 11, 1984.

398. AM is the author of *The Canadians*, 1985.

399. JC on "The Tonight Show," November 20, 1984.

404. Thanks to Gary Muldoon.

406. Thanks to Harry Roach.

410. SP is a standup comedian.

412. Quoted by Leah Garchik in the *San Francisco Chronicle*, December 6, 1985.

420–421. Quoted in *The Hollywood Hall of Shame* by Harry and Michael Medved, 1984.

422. Screenplay by Billy Wilder, Lesser Samuels, and Walter Newman.

423. Quoted in *The Jewish Mother's Hall of Fame*, by Fred Bernstein, 1986.

428. Thanks to Marty Indik.

430. SW on "The Tonight Show," February 28, 1985.

437. BM is a standup comedian.

442. Wording by RB.

451. JP in a letter to RB.

455. AB in *The Devil's Dictionary*.

456. EK at the opening of an exhibition of jade in January 1985.

462. CC to Ethel Barrymore, according to *Time*, March 6, 1955.

463. Screenplay by Jim Abrahams and Jim and Jerry Zucker.

464. Thanks to Tom Stewart.

465. RN during an interview on CBS in 1984.

470. See note 99.

473. Al Ordover is a close personal friend of Knox Burger.

474. RS is former chairman of the Democratic party.

477. FD in *Sports Illustrated*, July 9, 1984.

478. From *The Cynic's Lexicon*, compiled by Jonathon Green, 1982.

480. Quoted by Richard Nixon to Barbara Walters, May 8, 1985.

487. JM in the introduction to Hemingway's *The Most Dangerous Summer*, 1985.

495. CC is book editor of the *San Jose Mercury-News*.

496. GV in *Oui*, April 1975.

499. GF in a letter to Ivan Turgenev, November 8, 1879.

500. Quoted by Shay Duffrin in his one-man show *Confessions of an Irish Rebel*, 1984.
504. TJ in a letter, 1819.
505. TL is the coach of the Los Angeles Dodgers.
507. OW in *The Critic as Artist*, 1890.
509. LA in the *Sunday Times*, London, February 28, 1962.
511. IC in her 1981 novel *The Shooting Party*.
513. Quoted by Thomas Fleming in the *New York Times Book Review*, January 6, 1985.
514. Thanks to Hugh Parker.
515. Quoted by Merla Zellerbach in the *San Francisco Chronicle*, December 21, 1982.
518. Quoted in *New York* magazine, July 8, 1974.
519. PA reviewing *The Other 637 Best Things Anybody Ever Said* in the *San Rafael Independent Journal*, March 21, 1985.
521. RD is chiefly known as the former roommate of Marty Indik, who himself is not particularly well known.
524. GV in the *New York Times*, February 4, 1973.
525. RB in the *New York Times*, June 18, 1968.
527. RR in the *San Francisco Examiner*, July 1, 1984.
531. Thanks to Harry Roach.
532. JH as quoted in the *Pacific Sun*, November 28, 1985.
533. GK in *Lake Wobegone Days*, 1985.
534. FL in *Metropolitan Life*, 1978.
540. AHW in the *New York Times*, 1968.
542. From *The Cynic's Lexicon*, compiled by Jonathon Green, 1982.
543. JB in *Affurisms*, 1869.
545. Thanks to Lee Simon.
546. WMH in a letter to RB.
552. Quoted by Rob Morse in the *San Francisco Examiner*, January 5, 1986.
554. JP in *Aphorisms*, privately printed in 1985.
556. Thanks to Arlene Heath.
558. Thanks to Marty Indik.
560. WS in *The Merchant of Venice*.
565. KEG in *The Well-Tempered Sentence*, 1984.
566. LMB in his syndicated column, May 5, 1985.

568. Thanks to David L. Huard.
569. GBS as quoted by Ulick O'Connor in *All the Olympians*, 1984.
570. GBS in a letter to H. G. Wells.
573. Quoted by Herb Caen in the *San Francisco Chronicle*, November 17, 1985.
577. Thanks to Robert Gordon.
579. BB as quoted by Shay Duffrin in his one-man show *Confessions of an Irish Rebel*.
581. Cartoon caption in the *New Yorker*, January 6, 1986.
582. WT is a professional ventriloquist.
584. Thanks to Jim Eason.
586. Steve Allen remembers this line from the 1930's. Letter to RB.
587. SK is a standup comedian.
588. SP is a standup comedian.
590. Thanks to Marty Indik.
594. As given in *The Dictionary of Humorous Economics*.
597. AC in *Notebooks*, 1965.
598. Quoted by Herb Caen in the *San Francisco Chronicle*, February 2, 1985.
601. AE as quoted in *The Book of Political Quotes*, compiled by Jonathon Green, 1982.
606. JB as quoted by Joe Franklin in his *Encyclopedia of Comedy*, 1979.
609. ERM as quoted by Harry Reasoner.
613. JS as quoted in *The Book of Political Quotes*, compiled by Jonathon Green, 1982.
616. JL is a standup comedian.
617. See note 99.
618. HLM in a letter. Thanks to Marty Indik.
619. Quoted by Herb Caen in the *San Francisco Chronicle*, May 19, 1983.
621. Thanks to Bob Engan.
624. WT is a ventriloquist.
626. From the movie *Gentlemen Prefer Blondes*, 1953.
627. SB in a lecture in San Francisco, November 1984.
634. Thanks to Oakley Hall.
637. SK is a standup comedian.

Index of Authors

Index of Subjects and Key Words

✦❀❁❀✦

ABOUT THE AUTHOR

Robert Byrne vows not to shave until he is accepted by polite society. Little is known about this prickly reclusive man beyond what he has revealed in publicity handouts, talk-show appearances, and five autobiographical novels. He refuses to be interviewed for this page without being paid. Negotiations are continuing.